# kids draw™

**PUPPIES & WOLVES**

## CHRISTOPHER HART

WATSON-GUPTILL PUBLICATIONS/NEW YORK

*For anyone who loves to draw*

Senior Editor: Candace Raney
Editors: Alisa Palazzo and Julie Mazur
Designers: Bob Fillie, Graphiti Design, Inc. and Sivan Earnest
Production Manager: Hector Campbell

First published in 2001 by
Watson-Guptill Publications,
a division of BPI Communications, Inc.,
770 Broadway, New York, N.Y. 10003
www.watsonguptill.com

Based on *How to Draw Dogs, Puppies & Wolves*,
published in 1998 by Watson-Guptill Publications

**Library of Congress Card Number: 00-111774**

Printed in Singapore

First printing, 2001

1 2 3 4 5 6 7 8 / 08 07 06 05 04 03 02 01

# CONTENTS

Introduction 5

Dog Basics 6

DRAWING THE HEAD
TURNING THE HEAD
CREATING EXPRESSIONS
THE EARS
DRAWING THE BODY—SIDE VIEW
DRAWING THE BODY—3/4 VIEW
THE TRICKY FRONT POSE

Dogs with Papers 14

COCKER SPANIEL
CLASSIC TERRIER
CHOW CHOW
COLLIE
DOBERMAN PINSCHER
GREAT DANE
BULLMASTIFF
GERMAN SHEPHERD
SAINT BERNARD
MALTESE
CHIHUAHUA
BULLDOG: KING OF THE CARTOON BAD GUYS
OLD ENGLISH SHEEPDOG
EXOTIC BREEDS

Anatomy and Other Cool Stuff 28

WHY DOGS' JOINTS BEND THE WAY THEY DO
USING THE SKELETON TO UNDERSTAND CONTOURS
THE UNDERLYING BONE STRUCTURE
HOW A DOG WALKS
HOW A DOG RUNS
THE REALISTIC RUN VS. THE CARTOON RUN
CRUSHING AND STRETCHING
CREATING FLOWING LINES
THE LINE OF ACTION
THE SPINE LINE

Puppies 40

THE SITTING POSITION
THE RUNNING PUPPY
TYPES OF PUPPIES
DRAWING BABY DOGS
MUTTS

Wolves 48

THE GROWL
THE WOLF IN WINTER
THE VILLAINOUS WOLF
THE MANGY WOLF
THE STANDING WOLF

And Now for Some Really Wacky 'Toons! 56

COPYING HUMAN POSTURE
COSTUMES
ACCESSORIES AND PARTIAL COSTUMES
THE COLLAR & LEASH HAIR SALON
HAIRSTYLES
DRAWING AND REDRAWING
BOYS AND GIRLS TOGETHER

Index 64

# INTRODUCTION

Storybooks, comic strips, and cartoon TV shows are packed with funny dogs. No doubt about it, dogs are an all-time favorite subject of cartoonists. They're not just our best friend, but one of our favorite animals to draw, too!

You've probably looked at dogs a zillion times, but do you know where their elbows are? Hmmm. Do you know where their heels are? Hmmm. How can you draw a dog if you don't know?

This book will teach you about all kinds of dogs, from Labs to German shepherds, from lovable mutts to pampered poodles, and everything in between. You'll learn to draw dogs in action and with lots of funny expressions. You'll even learn how to give your dogs costumes and hilarious hairdos! Best of all, you'll learn how to create your own dog characters.

Along the way, you'll pick up some important drawing skills, like how to build drawings with simple shapes and how to use the "line of action." So if you're ready to have a doggone good time, fetch a pencil, get some paper, and let's get started!

# DOG BASICS

**A**ll dogs, no matter what breed, have the same basic head and body construction. Just master some basic steps and you'll be able to draw any type of dog!

## Drawing the Head

Let's start with a dalmatian, shown on the right.

1. Begin with a circle. Add two lines—one horizontal, one vertical. These are called *guidelines.* They will help you place the features.

2. The head has three basic parts: the skull, the cheeks, and the jaw.

3. Put the eyes on the horizontal "eye line."

4. Add the bridge of the nose. Notice how the nose gets larger as it comes toward you.

5. Add a smiling mouth. The mouth pushes up the cheeks to cause smile lines.

6. Big, floppy ears and a thick neck bring this guy to life.

7. Add the spots. Now erase your guidelines and you've got it!

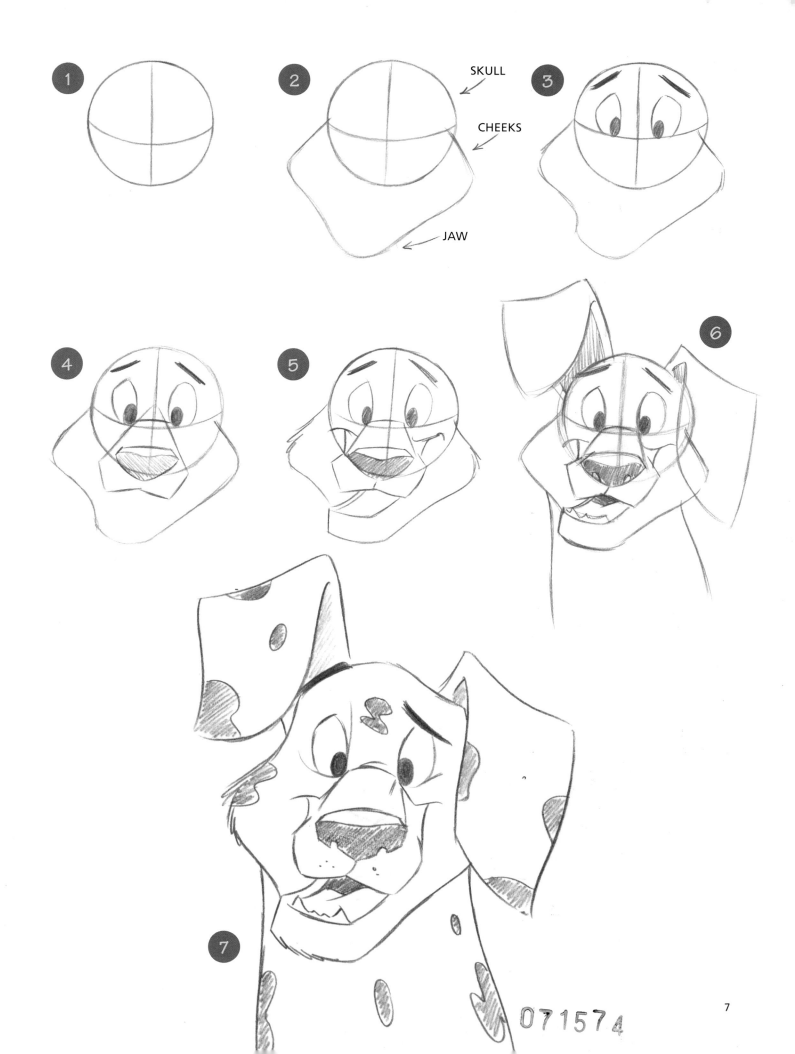

SKULL

CHEEKS

JAW

071574

7

# Turning the Head

Here are the most popular, basic angles of the cartoon dog's head.

FRONT VIEW

SIDE VIEW

3/4 VIEW

# Creating Expressions

Most people only think to use the mouth and eyebrows to create facial expressions. But there's more to it than that! You can change the shape of the eyes, for example, or the length of the upper lip. Practice the expressions below. Then try some of your own.

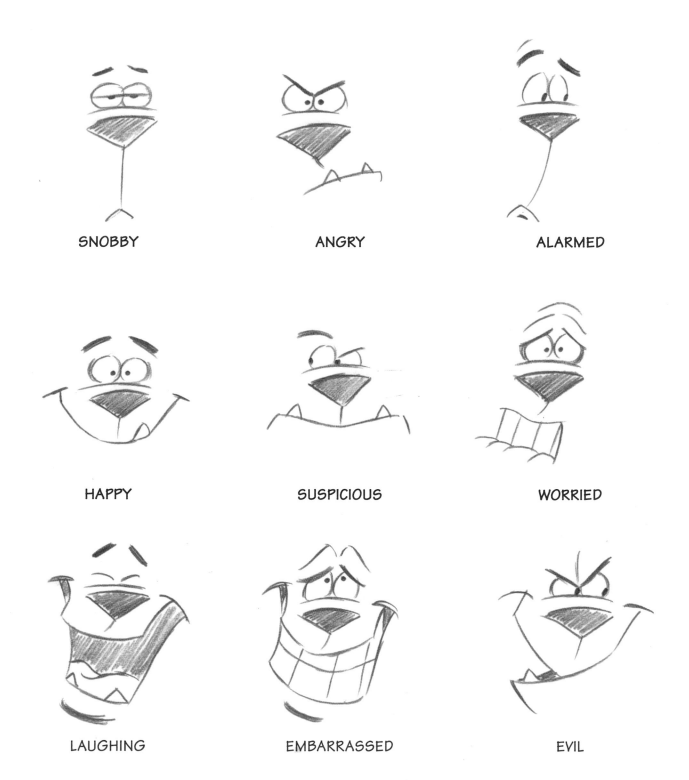

SNOBBY

ANGRY

ALARMED

HAPPY

SUSPICIOUS

WORRIED

LAUGHING

EMBARRASSED

EVIL

# The Ears

Human ears are on the side of the head. But dogs' ears are near the top, just off to the side.

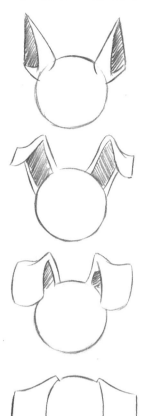

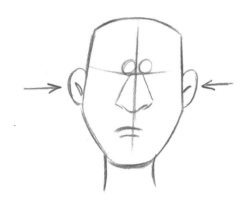

## FOLDED EARS
Most dog ears fold over, except for the short, triangular ears on terriers, chow chows, German shepherds, and a few other breeds.

**AN ASSORTMENT OF EARS**

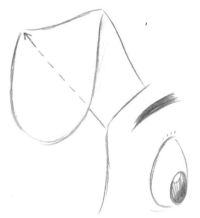

**RIGHT**
*The bottom line of the ear meets up with the outside corner.*

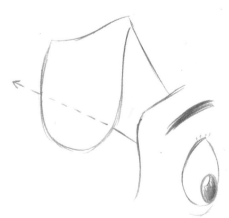

**WRONG**
*The bottom line of the ear just shoots out into space.*

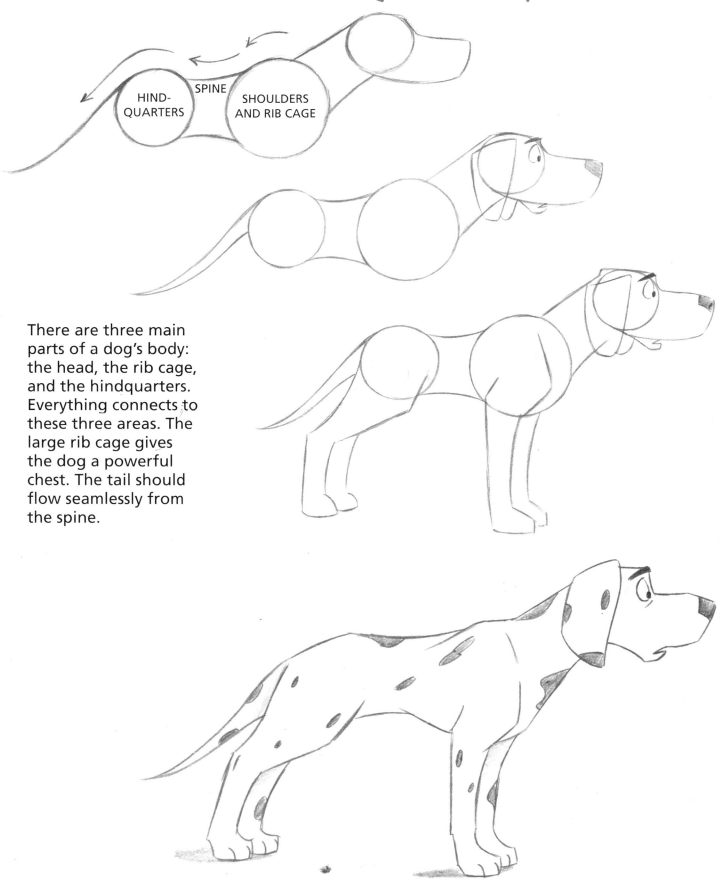

SPINE

HIND-QUARTERS

SHOULDERS AND RIB CAGE

There are three main parts of a dog's body: the head, the rib cage, and the hindquarters. Everything connects to these three areas. The large rib cage gives the dog a powerful chest. The tail should flow seamlessly from the spine.

# Drawing the Body—3/4 View

The law of *perspective* says that objects closer to us will look larger than objects farther away. In the 3/4 view, the rib cage is closer to us than the hindquarters, so it should appear larger.

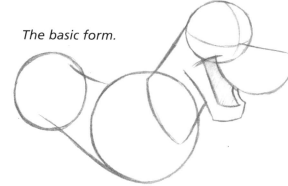

*The basic form.*

*Add some character to the face. Start drawing the front legs.*

*The feet aren't round—they have sides to them.*

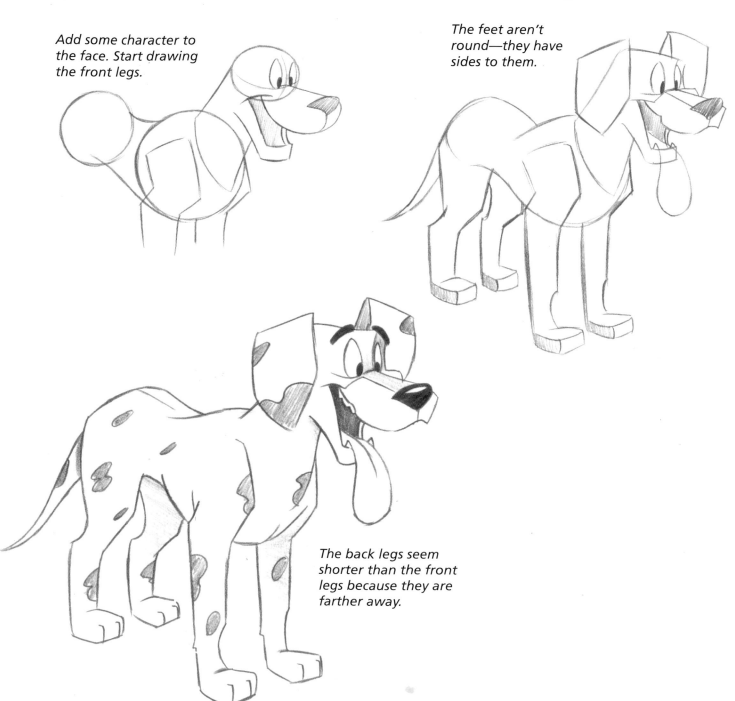

*The back legs seem shorter than the front legs because they are farther away.*

When drawing a dog from the front, turn him just a bit to the side while keeping his head facing front. This way, parts of the body will overlap to create a sense of depth. This will help the dog look round and real instead of flat and fake.

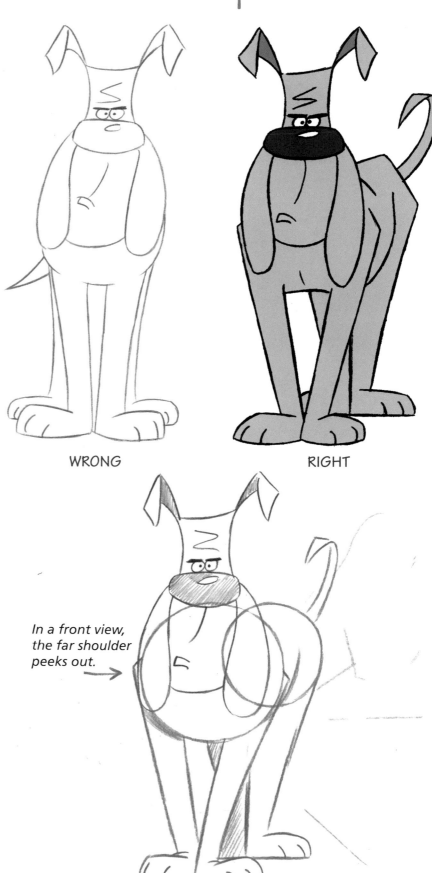

WRONG                    RIGHT

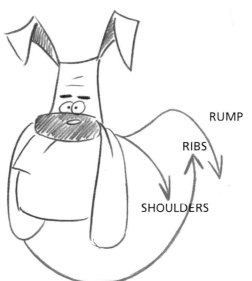

RUMP

RIBS

SHOULDERS

*Notice the overlapping lines.*

*In a front view, the far shoulder peeks out.* →

# DOGS WITH PAPERS

**T**hese are the classic dogs you see in the movies and the funnies— and maybe in your own backyard! Use what you've already learned to work through this section.

## Cocker Spaniel

Real dogs usually don't like sweets, but cartoon dogs eat everything, especially dessert! The cocker spaniel is a loyal pet. It is shaggy but not messy-looking. It loves the outdoors, as well as a warm, cozy home.

UNDERLYING STRUCTURE

The terrier's neck is thick and muscular. His little body is very sturdy. And short legs keep him just above the ground. He's got bushy eyebrows, a bushy mouth, bushy legs, and small paws. Notice his triangle-shaped ears. And look at his small bottom teeth. Terriers started out as hunting dogs before getting used to indoor heat and Nintendo.

# Chow Chow

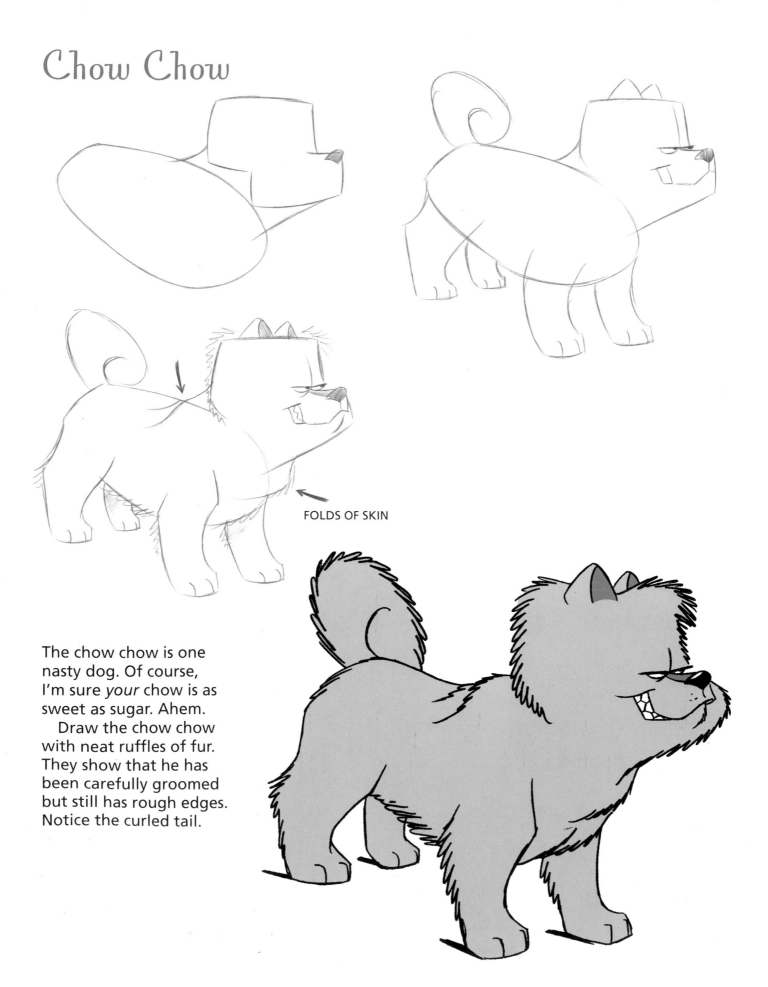

The chow chow is one nasty dog. Of course, I'm sure *your* chow is as sweet as sugar. Ahem.

Draw the chow chow with neat ruffles of fur. They show that he has been carefully groomed but still has rough edges. Notice the curled tail.

FOLDS OF SKIN

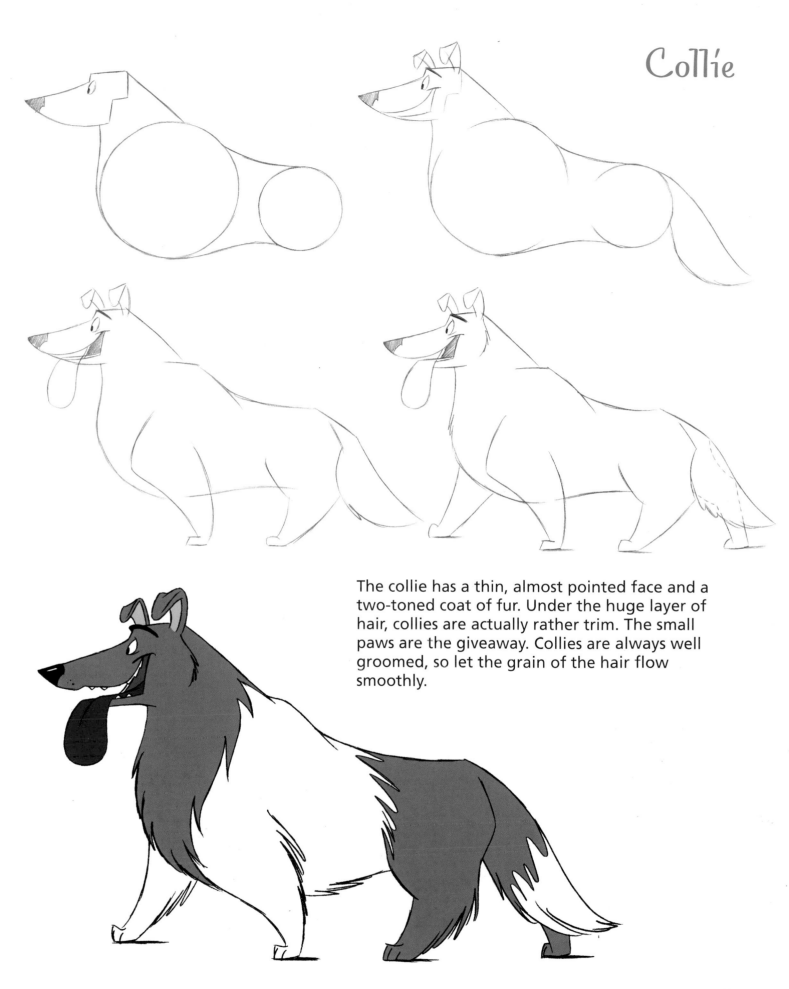

# Collie

The collie has a thin, almost pointed face and a two-toned coat of fur. Under the huge layer of hair, collies are actually rather trim. The small paws are the giveaway. Collies are always well groomed, so let the grain of the hair flow smoothly.

# Doberman Pinscher

These dogs look tough, thanks to their large chests and narrow hips. They also have small skulls, flat foreheads, and thick, muscular necks. Note the short tail. Dobermans are always either reddish brown and black or just reddish brown.

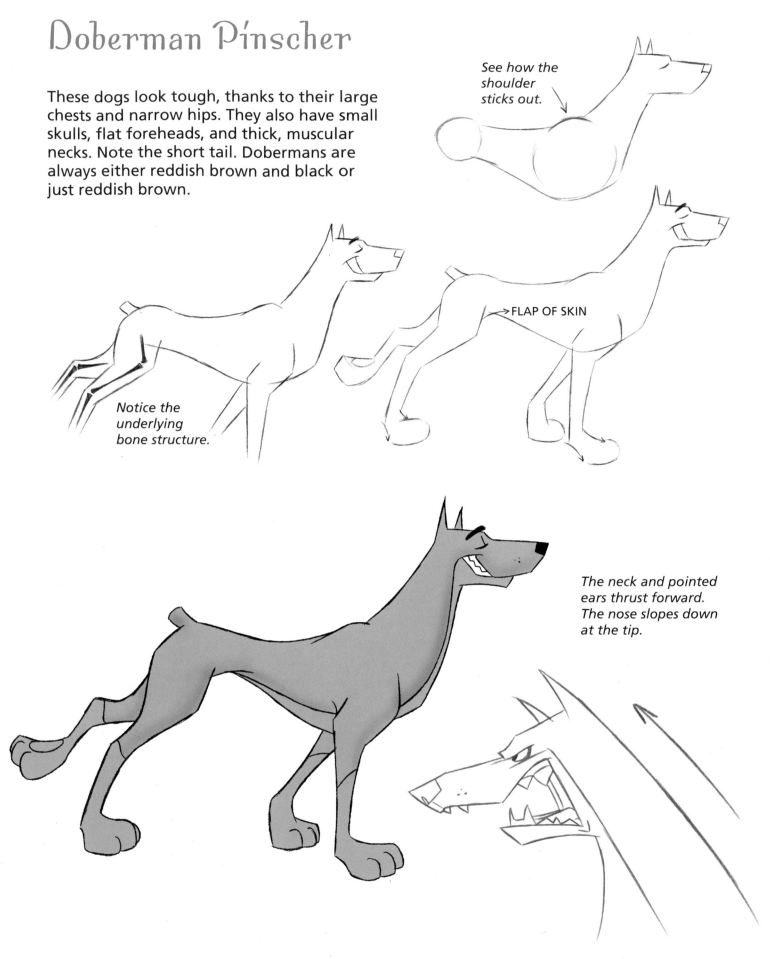

See how the shoulder sticks out.

Notice the underlying bone structure.

→ FLAP OF SKIN

The neck and pointed ears thrust forward. The nose slopes down at the tip.

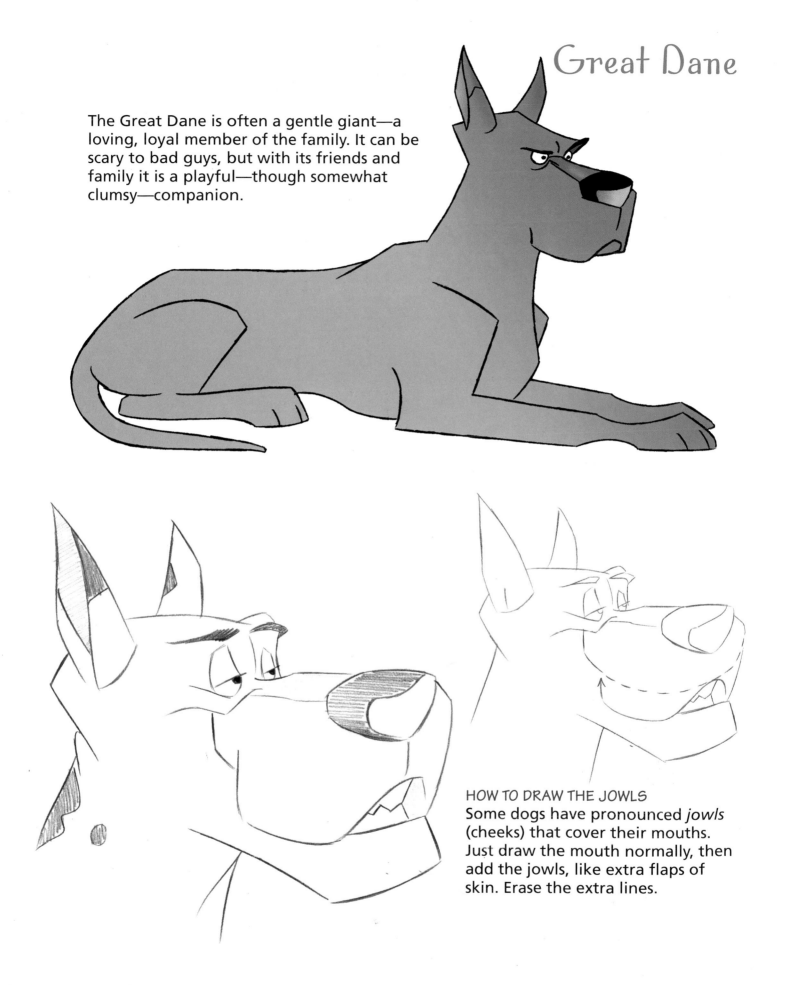

# Great Dane

The Great Dane is often a gentle giant—a loving, loyal member of the family. It can be scary to bad guys, but with its friends and family it is a playful—though somewhat clumsy—companion.

HOW TO DRAW THE JOWLS
Some dogs have pronounced *jowls* (cheeks) that cover their mouths. Just draw the mouth normally, then add the jowls, like extra flaps of skin. Erase the extra lines.

# Bullmastiff

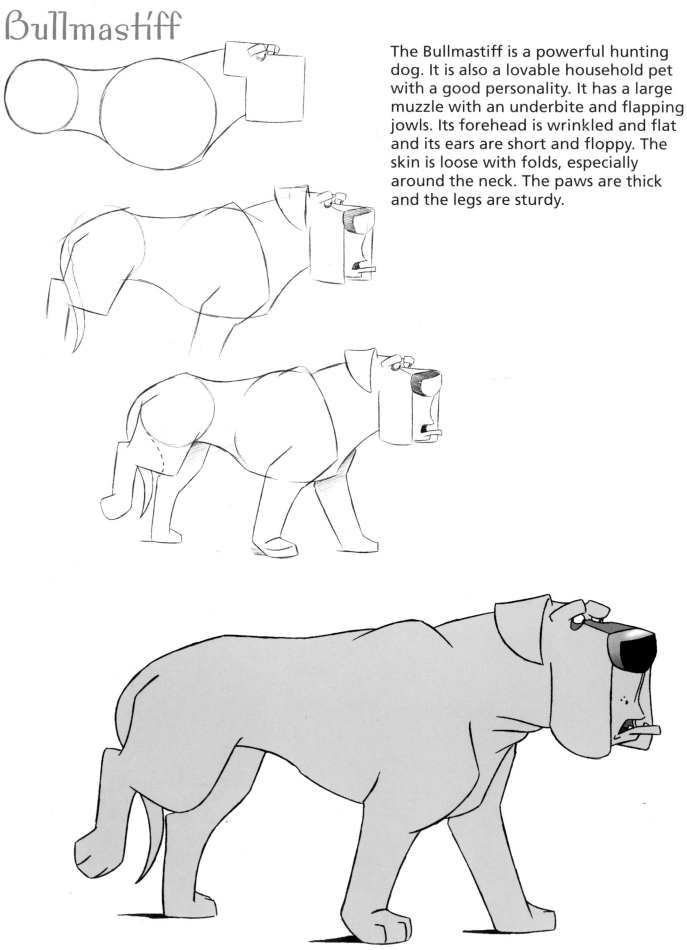

The Bullmastiff is a powerful hunting dog. It is also a lovable household pet with a good personality. It has a large muzzle with an underbite and flapping jowls. Its forehead is wrinkled and flat and its ears are short and floppy. The skin is loose with folds, especially around the neck. The paws are thick and the legs are sturdy.

# German Shepherd

This breed was a police dog in World War II. It has black, triangular ears. Sometimes it has markings around the eyes like a mask. Sprinkle black patches along its back and legs.

In a sneaking pose, the upper body slinks low to the ground while the hindquarters rise.

# Saint Bernard

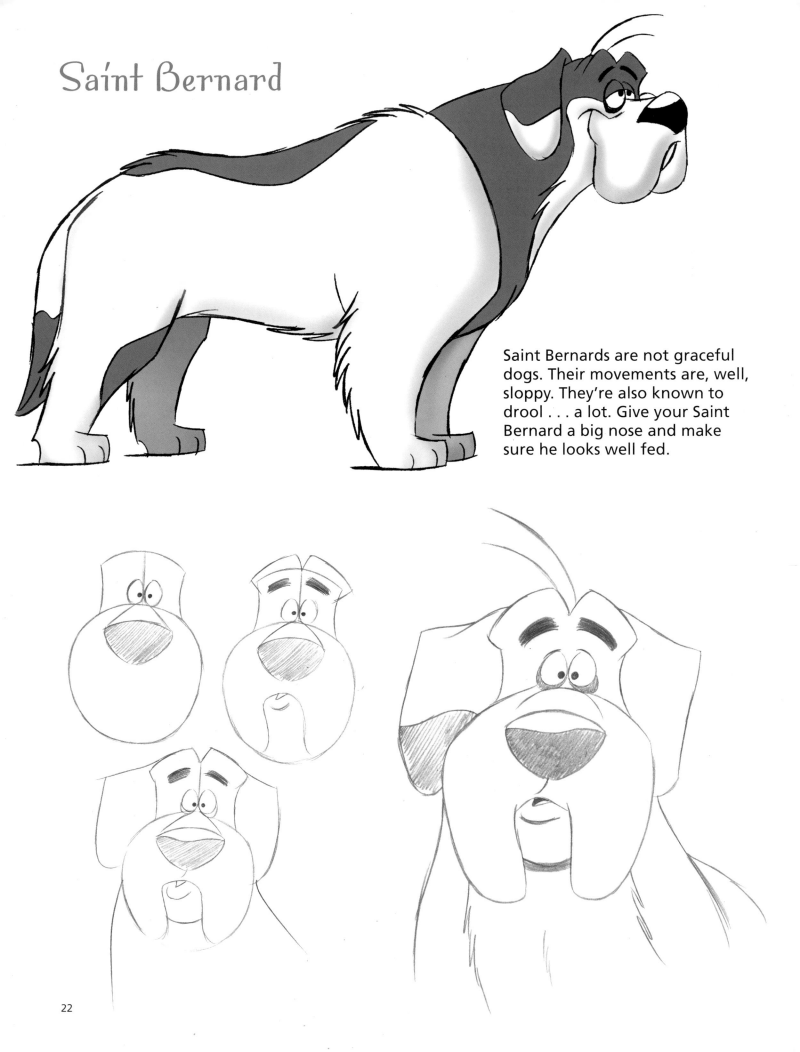

Saint Bernards are not graceful dogs. Their movements are, well, sloppy. They're also known to drool . . . a lot. Give your Saint Bernard a big nose and make sure he looks well fed.

# Maltese

These dogs are pampered. They have ridiculously long haircuts and often wear ribbons, or even jewelry. They might also wear designer doggy clothes, as they get cold easily.

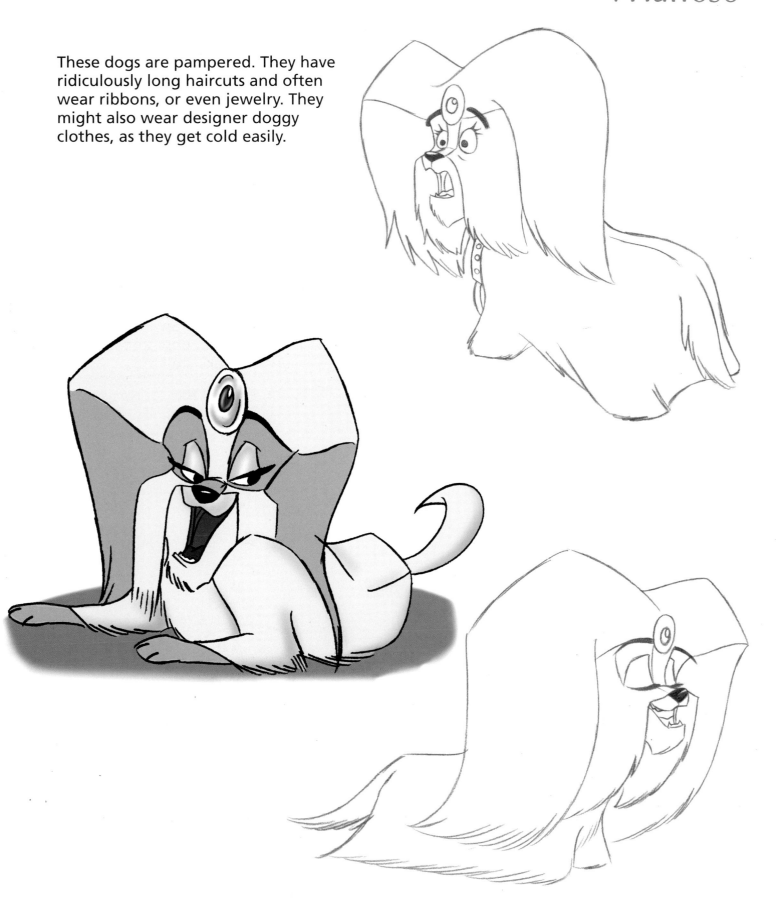

# Chihuahua

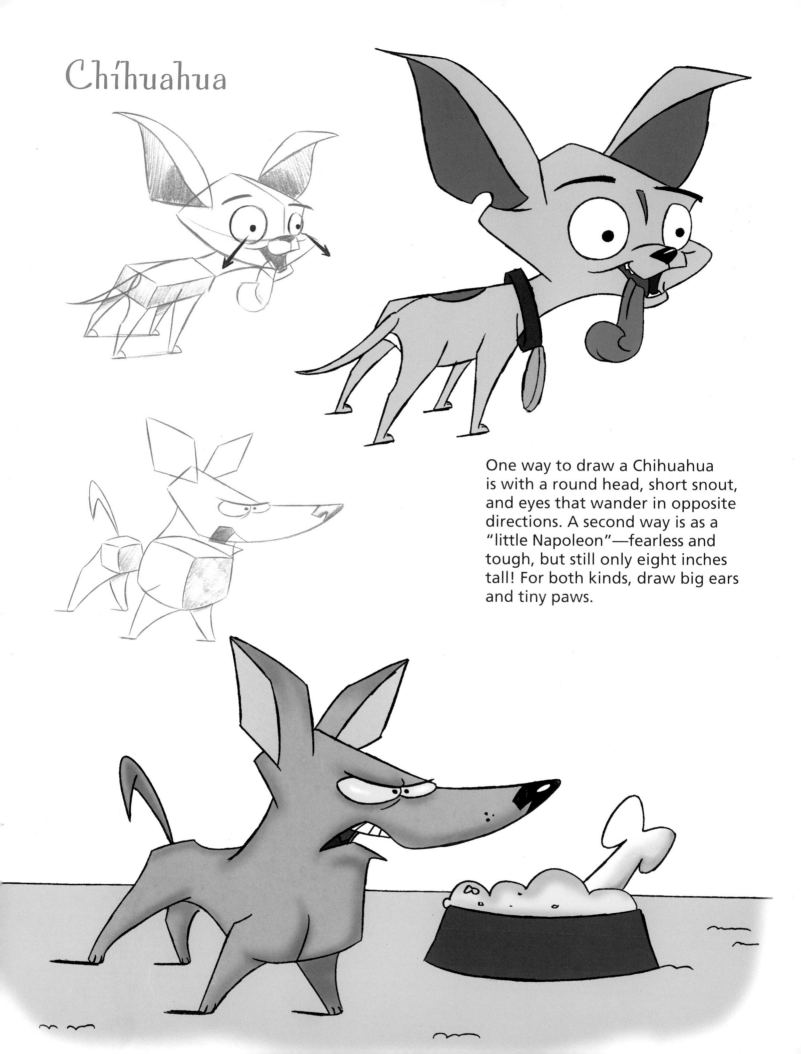

One way to draw a Chihuahua is with a round head, short snout, and eyes that wander in opposite directions. A second way is as a "little Napoleon"—fearless and tough, but still only eight inches tall! For both kinds, draw big ears and tiny paws.

# Bulldog: King of the Cartoon Bad Guys

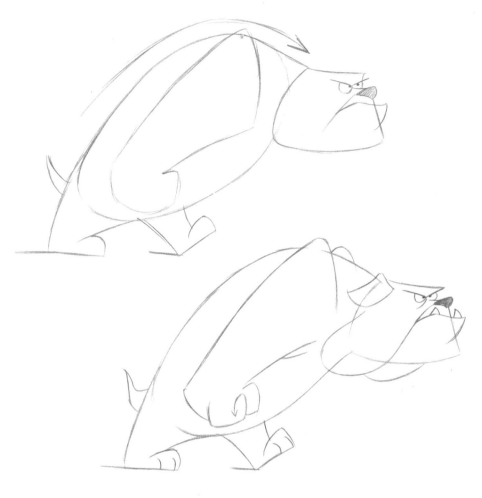

Here is the character you love to hate. Put the bulldog in a cartoon and you immediately know whom to root *against*!

Bulldogs have massive, wrinkled eyebrows and huge chins. They're also famous for their gigantic jowls.

**THE BULLDOG'S BODY**
*When shown standing, the cartoon bulldog is quite tall. (A real bulldog is actually very short.) It has a massive chest and shoulders, but only itsy-bitsy hind legs. Its tiny tail is short and crooked.*

# Old English Sheepdog

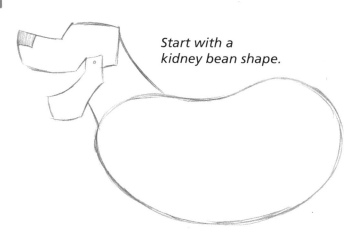

Start with a kidney bean shape.

*Since the eyes are hidden, I like showing the teeth.*

Never, ever show the eyes of a sheepdog! They should always be under a floppy mound of hair. The sheepdog's body is also hidden under that shaggy carpet.

*Draw the legs with soft, rounded angles.*

*Add shaggy hair to the underbelly.*

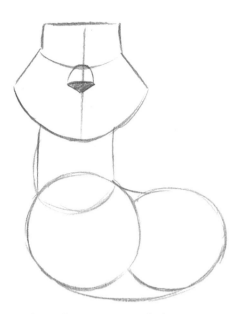

Try drawing some of the more exotic breeds, especially those from foreign countries. Most people won't recognize these dogs, so you can be freer in designing them.

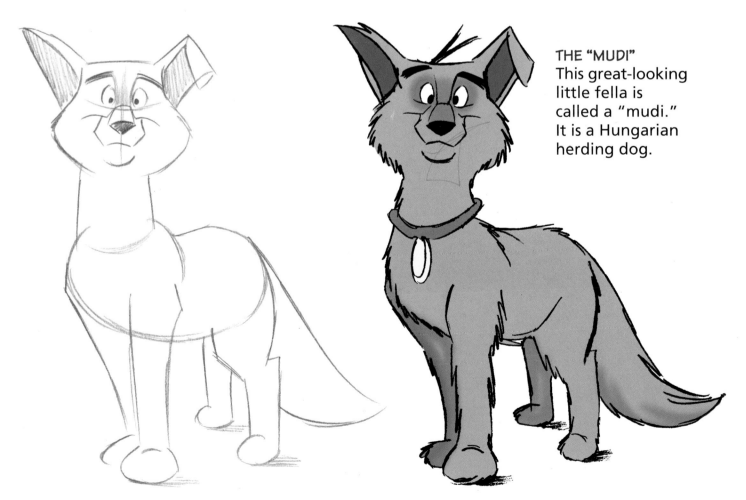

**THE "MUDI"**
This great-looking little fella is called a "mudi." It is a Hungarian herding dog.

# ANATOMY AND OTHER COOL STUFF

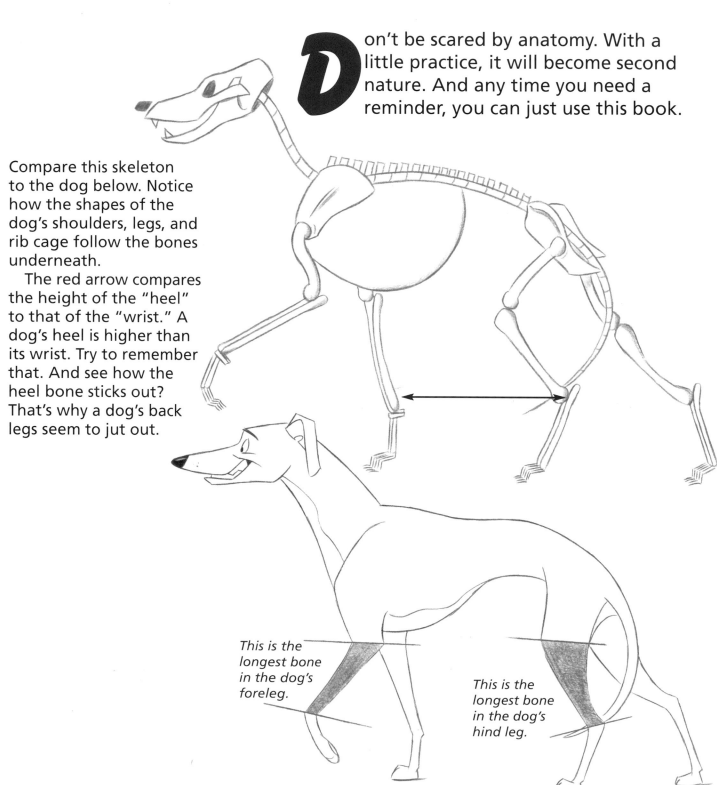

**D**on't be scared by anatomy. With a little practice, it will become second nature. And any time you need a reminder, you can just use this book.

Compare this skeleton to the dog below. Notice how the shapes of the dog's shoulders, legs, and rib cage follow the bones underneath.

The red arrow compares the height of the "heel" to that of the "wrist." A dog's heel is higher than its wrist. Try to remember that. And see how the heel bone sticks out? That's why a dog's back legs seem to jut out.

This is the longest bone in the dog's foreleg.

This is the longest bone in the dog's hind leg.

# Why Dogs' Joints Bend the Way They Do

Dogs don't walk on their "hands" and "feet." Dogs walk on their fingers and toes. That's right. Their heels stick up in the air when they walk or stand. This is how a person would have to walk if he or she were to walk like a dog.

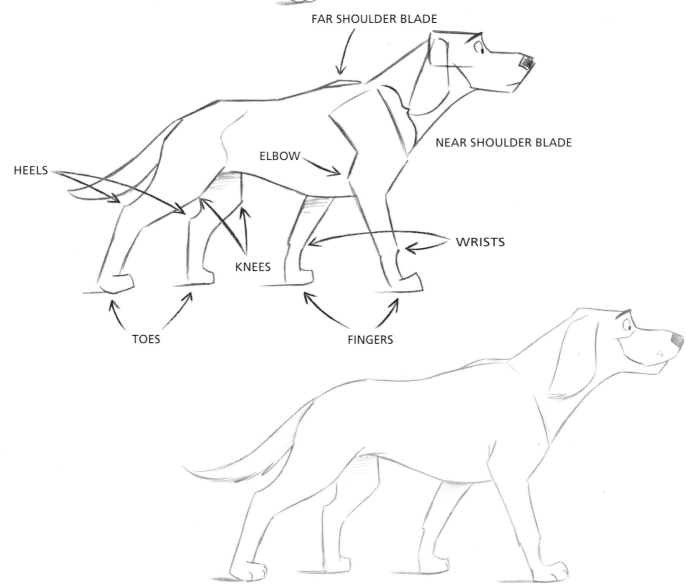

FAR SHOULDER BLADE

NEAR SHOULDER BLADE

ELBOW

HEELS

KNEES

WRISTS

TOES

FINGERS

# Using the Skeleton to Understand Contours

Contour lines are lines that show on the body. You can see countour lines around a dog's hips and shoulders.

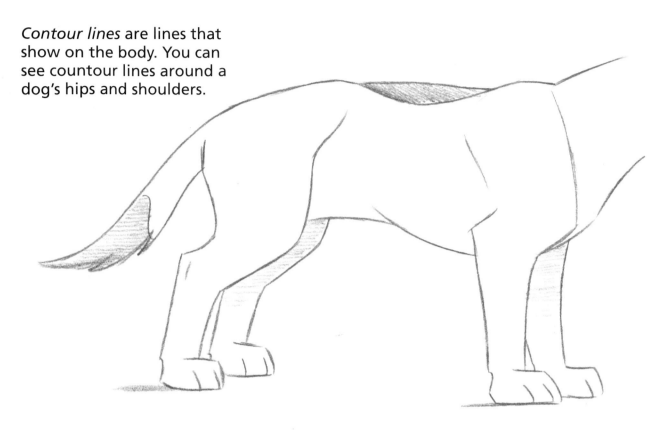

CONTOUR LINES FOLLOW
THE SKELETON UNDERNEATH

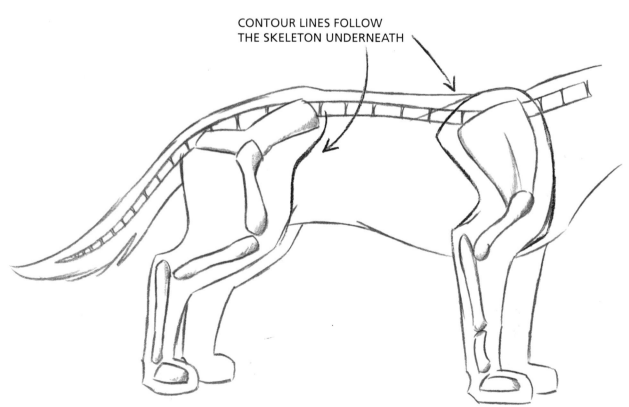

# The Underlying Bone Structure

Here is a simple rule to help you. The dog's shoulder blades and pelvis slope out like the two sides of a triangle. (Look at the dotted lines in this picture.) If you can remember this, it will be easier to place the legs.

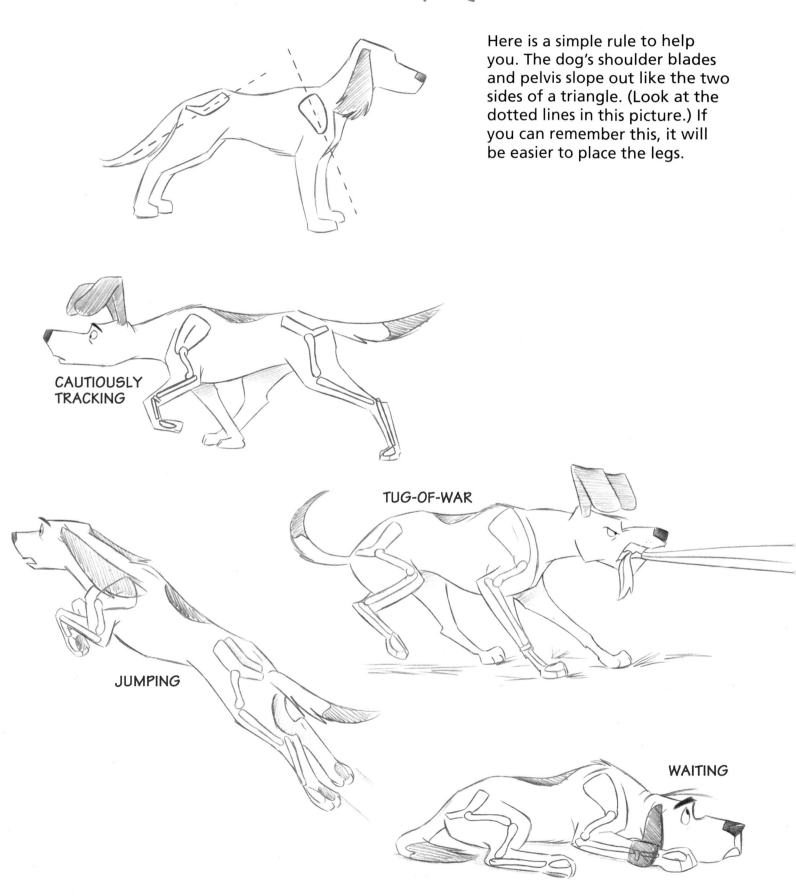

CAUTIOUSLY TRACKING

TUG-OF-WAR

JUMPING

WAITING

# How a Dog Walks

A dog steps with a hind leg first. When that hind leg hits the ground, the foreleg on the *same* side takes a forward step.

It's that simple. Back leg, front leg on the same side. Then back leg, front leg on the other side.

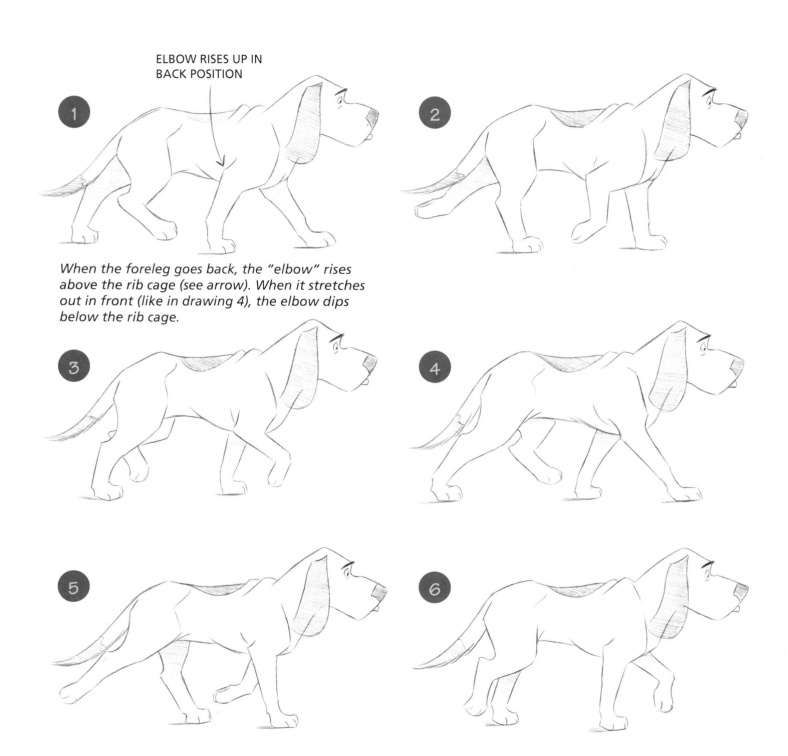

ELBOW RISES UP IN BACK POSITION

*When the foreleg goes back, the "elbow" rises above the rib cage (see arrow). When it stretches out in front (like in drawing 4), the elbow dips below the rib cage.*

# How a Dog Runs

When dogs run, they place their feet in order, one after the other. If the dog begins by landing on its right foreleg, it would then land on its left foreleg, then on its left hind leg, and then on its right hind leg. Then it starts all over again with the right foreleg. Try to follow the sequence in the pictures below.

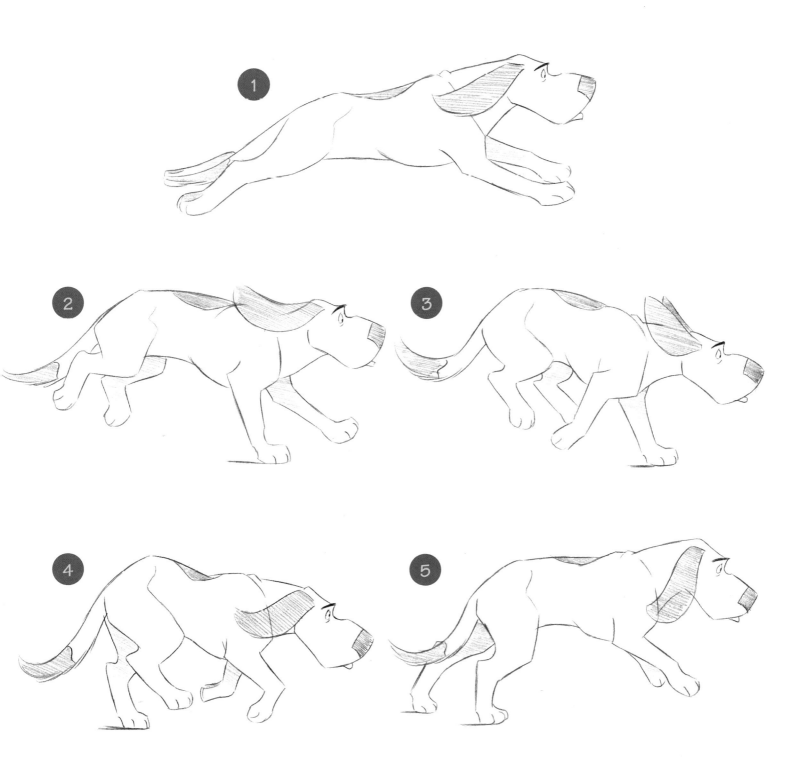

# The Realistic Run vs. the Cartoon Run

**REALISTIC RUN**
This greyhound is shown running realistically.

**WACKY RUN**
You don't have to play by the rules. This wackier dog is doing a completely made-up, silly run. A real dog's hind legs could never go up this high. That's what makes the pose so funny.

When a dog walks, its shoulders and hips sway from left to right. This makes it look like one side of the body is moving together (*crushing*) and the other side is *stretching*. Watch a real dog walk to see how this works.

*This dog's right foreleg is back, so his head and shoulders sway to the right. His left hind leg is also back, so his hips sway to the left. The left side of his body is stretching and the right side is crushing.*

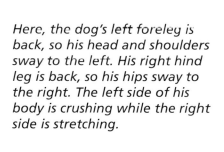

*Here, the dog's left foreleg is back, so his head and shoulders sway to the left. His right hind leg is back, so his hips sway to the right. The left side of his body is crushing while the right side is stretching.*

35

# Creating Flowing Lines

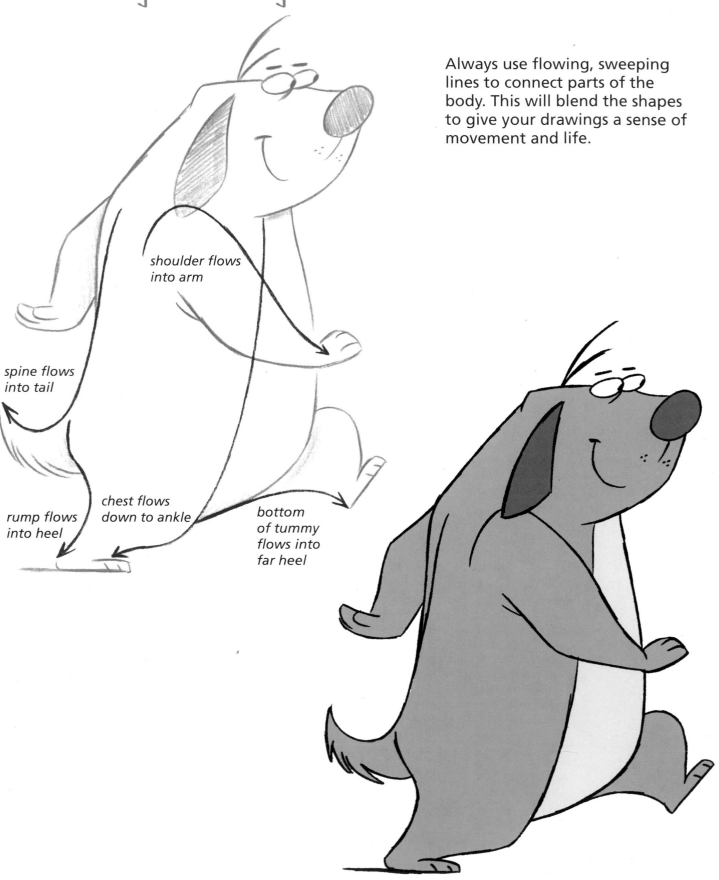

Always use flowing, sweeping lines to connect parts of the body. This will blend the shapes to give your drawings a sense of movement and life.

*shoulder flows into arm*

*spine flows into tail*

*rump flows into heel*

*chest flows down to ankle*

*bottom of tummy flows into far heel*

# The Line of Action

Your drawings should have an overall flow. This is where the *line of action* comes into play. The line of action is a single, sweeping line that sets the direction of your character's pose. Look at the example below.

LINE OF ACTION

Always start with a line of
action, even if your character
is just sitting or standing still.
The line can be straight or
bendy, depending on the pose.
Here are a few examples.

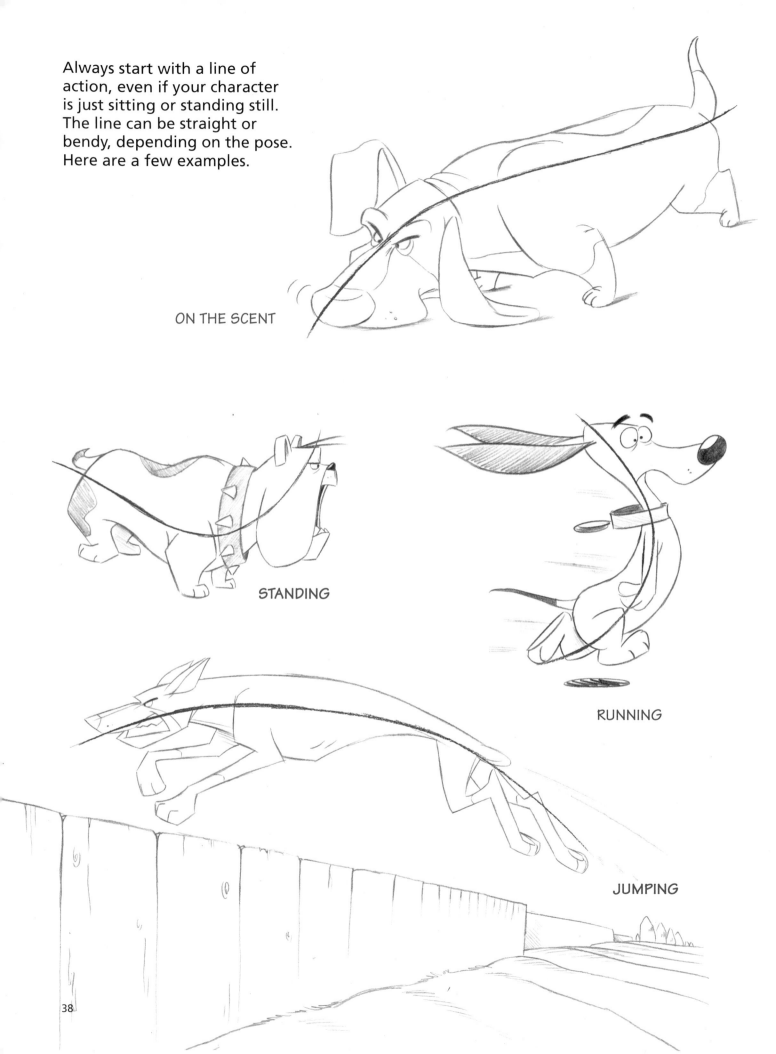

ON THE SCENT

STANDING

RUNNING

JUMPING

# The Spine Line

A dog's spine is very close to the skin. You can even see it a little. Show the line of the spine as it curves around the back. This will help the back look round.

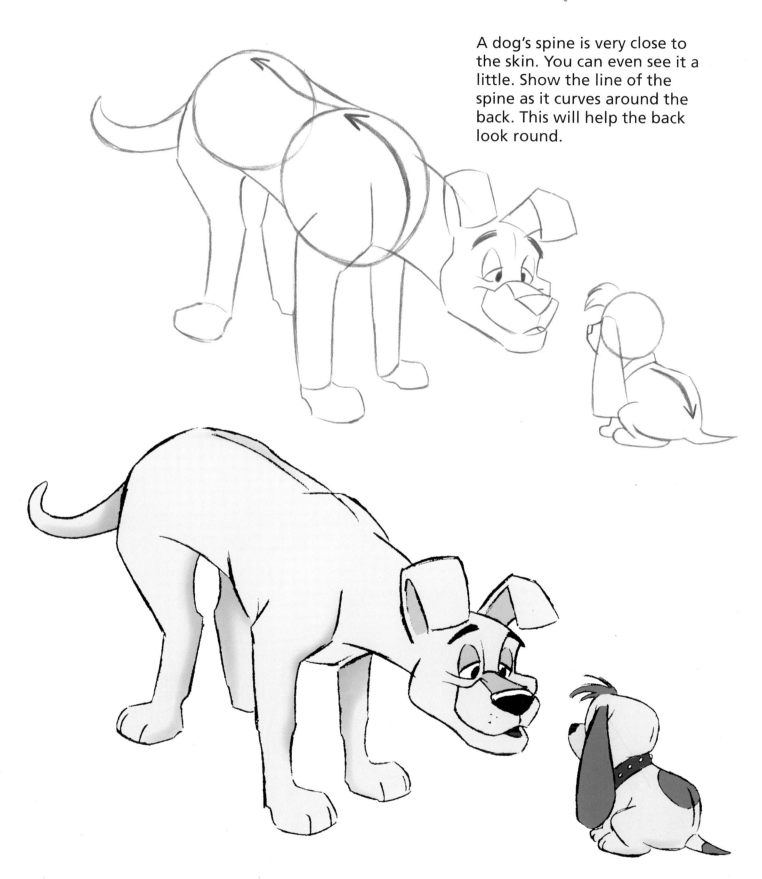

# PUPPIES

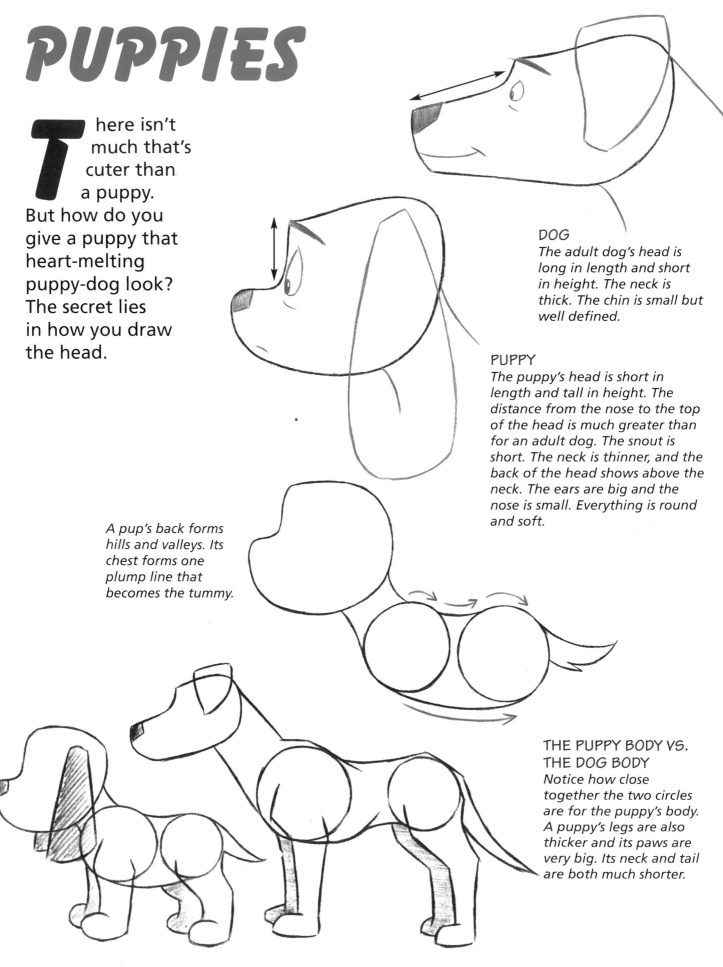

There isn't much that's cuter than a puppy. But how do you give a puppy that heart-melting puppy-dog look? The secret lies in how you draw the head.

**DOG**
*The adult dog's head is long in length and short in height. The neck is thick. The chin is small but well defined.*

**PUPPY**
*The puppy's head is short in length and tall in height. The distance from the nose to the top of the head is much greater than for an adult dog. The snout is short. The neck is thinner, and the back of the head shows above the neck. The ears are big and the nose is small. Everything is round and soft.*

*A pup's back forms hills and valleys. Its chest forms one plump line that becomes the tummy.*

**THE PUPPY BODY VS. THE DOG BODY**
*Notice how close together the two circles are for the puppy's body. A puppy's legs are also thicker and its paws are very big. Its neck and tail are both much shorter.*

# The Sitting Position

The sitting position is especially cute for a puppy.

**WRONG**
*A real dog's back would never slope this way while sitting.*

**RIGHT**
*This is correct. The back should arch outward.*

# The Running Puppy

Notice how the ears flap back during the run. A puppy runs with a floppy joy.

Try changing things like the ears, hairstyle, and eyes to create all kinds of puppy characters.

THE MISCHIEVOUS PUP
The standing puppy has a pear-shaped torso.

*A centerline will help you place features on the head.*

THE BULLY
The bulldog pup is just as mean as the adult! Notice how the front paws turn inward—this is unique to the bulldog. Also notice the size of the head. The head must be much larger than the rest of the body for it to look like a puppy.

**THE BRAINY PUP**
Smart pups can have glasses and high foreheads. They are usually on the wimpy side, too.

# Drawing Baby Dogs

Dog babies are drawn differently from puppies. They have short ears, whereas pups have long ears. And the head is even bigger compared to the body. They are usually drawn in diapers and with things like bottles, ribbons, and rattles.

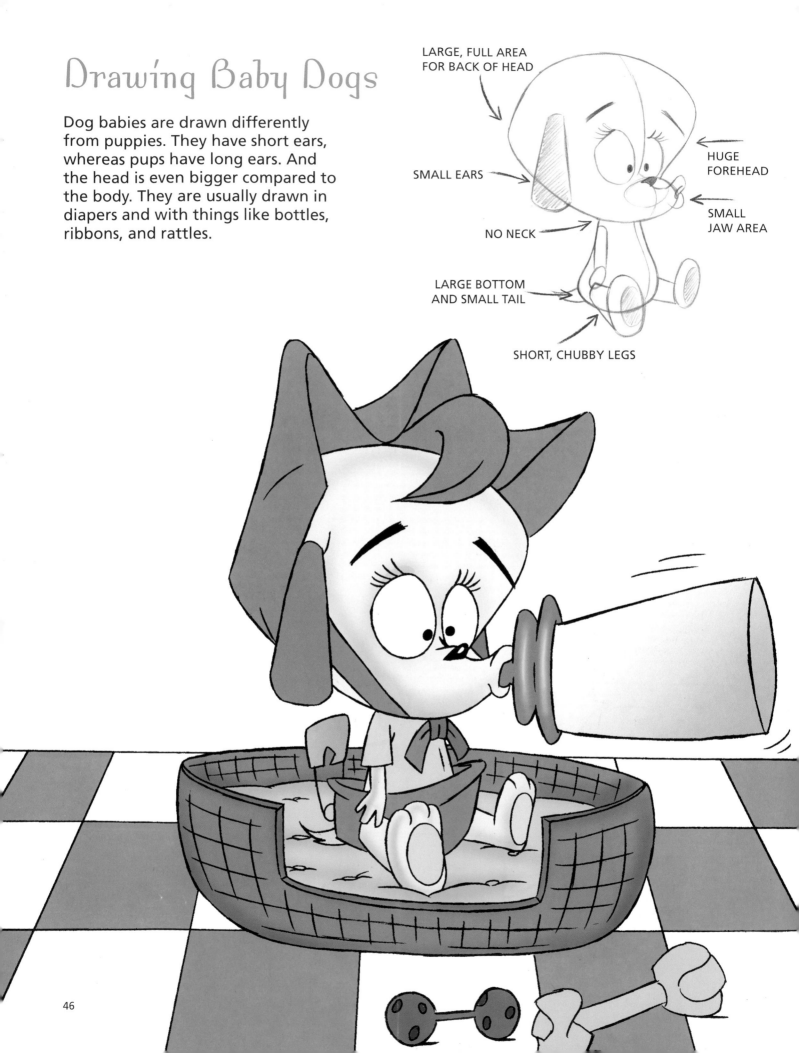

LARGE, FULL AREA FOR BACK OF HEAD

SMALL EARS

HUGE FOREHEAD

SMALL JAW AREA

NO NECK

LARGE BOTTOM AND SMALL TAIL

SHORT, CHUBBY LEGS

There are no rules when drawing mutts. You can create something strange, or just a scruffy, average dog. You might try adding a large ring around one eye, or giving an otherwise white dog black ears and a black tail.

# WOLVES

**A**ll dogs, from the largest to the smallest, evolved from wolves. I love to draw wolves because they can play so many roles, from scary villains to wacky cartoon types or cool hipsters.

Here is a dog (top), fox (middle), and wolf (bottom). The wolf is the size of a large dog. It is thinner and has longer legs. Its tail hangs low to the ground. It has a furry appearance, a long snout, and large, pointy ears. Its tail is large and fluffy. It has delicate limbs with special markings and tiny paws.

# The Growl

There is nothing more frightening than staring down a wolf that's baring its teeth at you!

**SIDE VIEW**
*The break in the bridge of the nose gives this wolf a ferocious look.*

**FRONT VIEW**

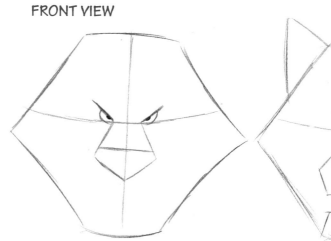

*Start with the basic shape of the wolf's head. Draw guidelines. Place the bridge of the nose where the guidelines meet. Notice how the eyebrows come out of the bridge of the nose.*

*The ears are almost perfect triangles. The muzzle is the same shape as for a dog. Leave extra space for the teeth.*

*Draw the top and bottom teeth. Add wrinkles on the bridge of the nose and ruffle up the fur a little. Add dark circles under the eyes.*

# The Wolf in Winter

See how slowly this wolf seems to be moving through the snow. You can *feel* him trudging with great effort. The head hangs low and the eyes are shut tight against the whipping winds. Notice that his fur and tail are shown blowing in the *same* direction as the wind.

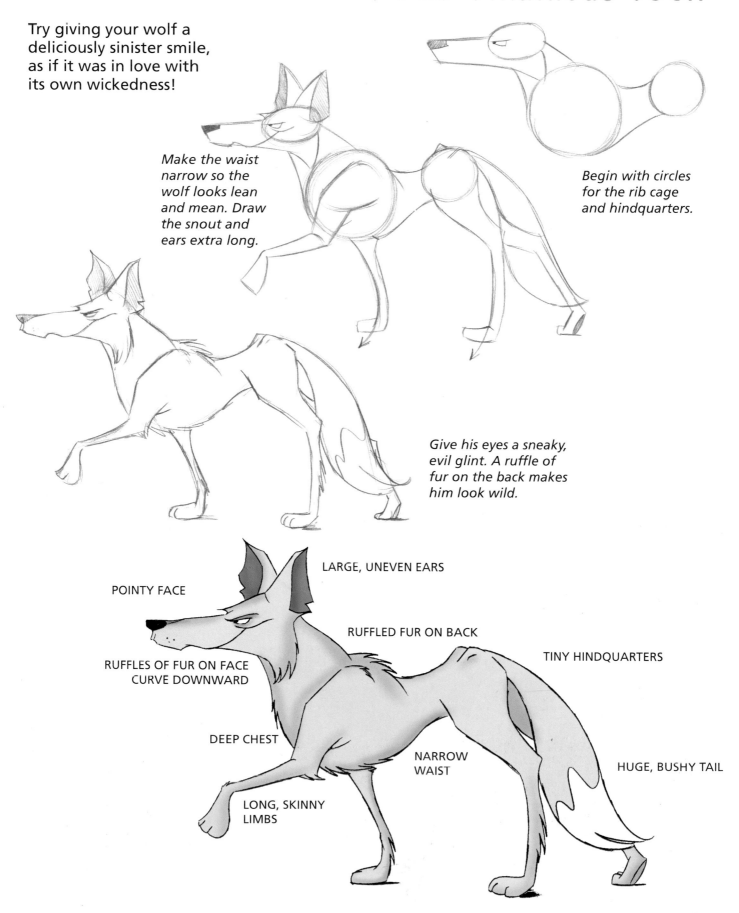

Try giving your wolf a deliciously sinister smile, as if it was in love with its own wickedness!

*Make the waist narrow so the wolf looks lean and mean. Draw the snout and ears extra long.*

*Begin with circles for the rib cage and hindquarters.*

*Give his eyes a sneaky, evil glint. A ruffle of fur on the back makes him look wild.*

POINTY FACE

LARGE, UNEVEN EARS

RUFFLED FUR ON BACK

TINY HINDQUARTERS

RUFFLES OF FUR ON FACE CURVE DOWNWARD

DEEP CHEST

NARROW WAIST

HUGE, BUSHY TAIL

LONG, SKINNY LIMBS

# The Mangy Wolf

For a mangy wolf, show the ribs with a few lines. The pelvis and shoulder blades should show through the skin. Draw the paws larger and the legs thinner than normal to make the wolf look even skinnier.

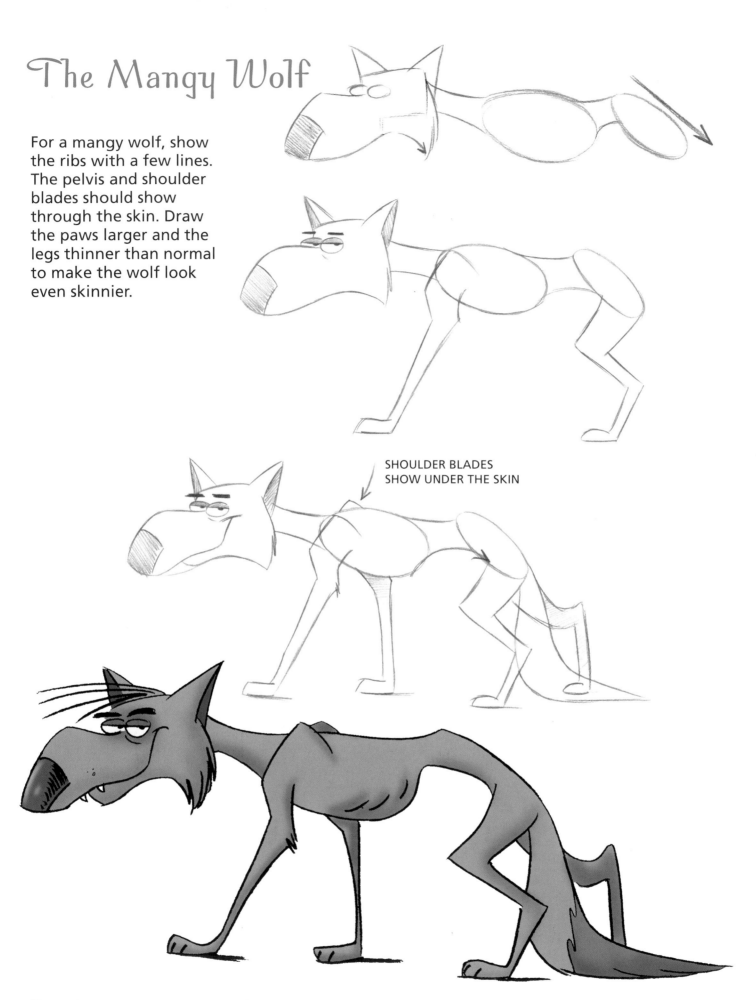

SHOULDER BLADES
SHOW UNDER THE SKIN

# The Standing Wolf

Not all wolves are threatening.
This one is a good example.
It stands like a person and has
hips wider than its chest.

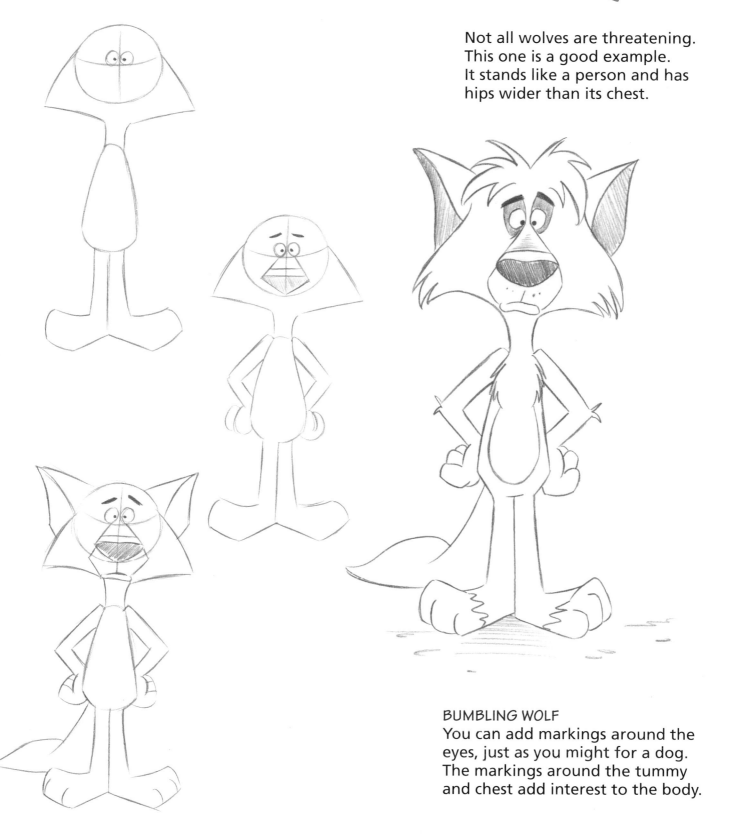

BUMBLING WOLF
You can add markings around the
eyes, just as you might for a dog.
The markings around the tummy
and chest add interest to the body.

### HOT-TEMPERED WOLF
In cartoons, bad guys always have heavy eyebrows. You can also put ruffles of fur at the elbows, tail, forehead, and chest.

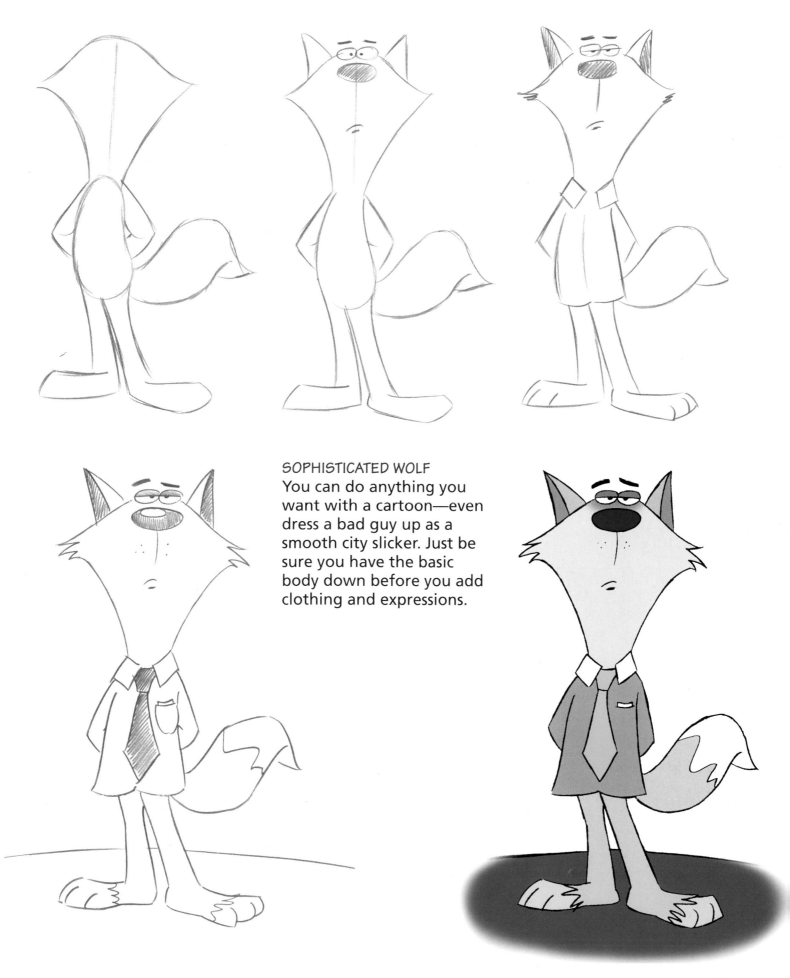

## SOPHISTICATED WOLF

You can do anything you want with a cartoon—even dress a bad guy up as a smooth city slicker. Just be sure you have the basic body down before you add clothing and expressions.

# AND NOW FOR SOME REALLY WACKY 'TOONS!

**H**ere are a few tricks to give your dogs, puppies, and wolves that extra punch. Whether it's adding a costume or simply tweaking your drawing style, you can always boost your characters' appeal.

You can draw a cartoon dog, puppy, or wolf standing naturally on all fours, or you can draw it standing upright, like a person. It's up to you.

**CARTOONY DOG**
*It's easy to transform this guy into a two-legged character.*

**MORE REALISTIC DOG**
*This dog is so realistic that posing him upright is not enough to make him look human. It's only by adding clothes that he becomes convincing.*

# Costumes

A costume can help show your dog's personality. It tells people what your character does for a job, or the types of hobbies it has.

*The costume tells us that this dog is a police officer.*

*The bulldog above is obviously a tough guy. But what does he do? Is he a dad, a bus driver, or a football coach? There's no way to tell. On the other hand, the bulldog at right is clearly a doorman. He'll have no trouble keeping out unwanted guests!*

# Accessories and Partial Costumes

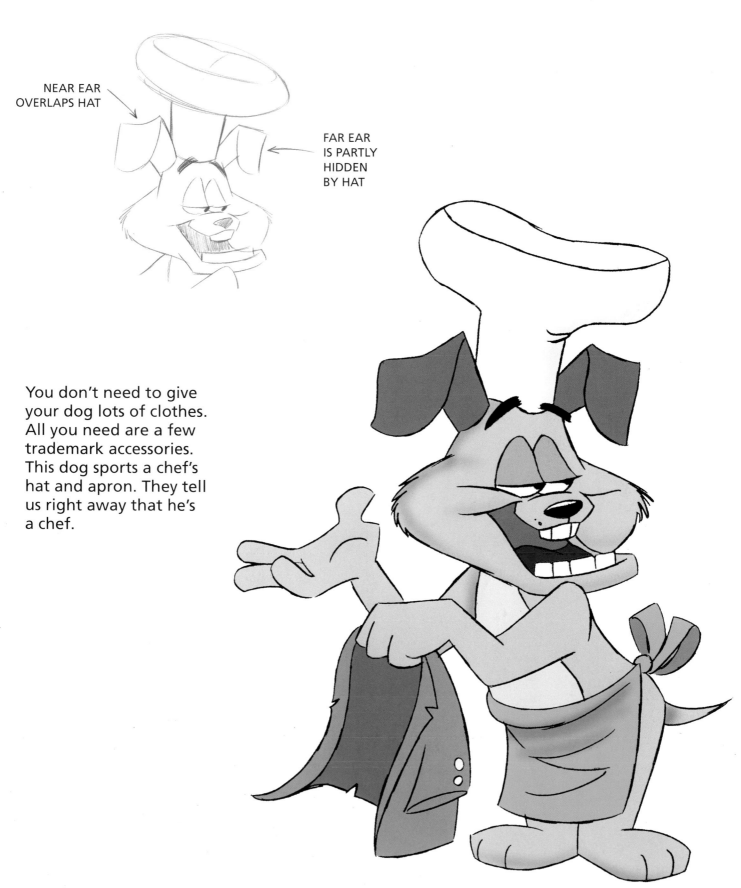

NEAR EAR
OVERLAPS HAT

FAR EAR
IS PARTLY
HIDDEN
BY HAT

You don't need to give your dog lots of clothes. All you need are a few trademark accessories. This dog sports a chef's hat and apron. They tell us right away that he's a chef.

# The Collar & Leash Hair Salon

Hairstyles will make your cartoon animals seem even more humanlike. Always draw the head shape first, then add the hairstyle.

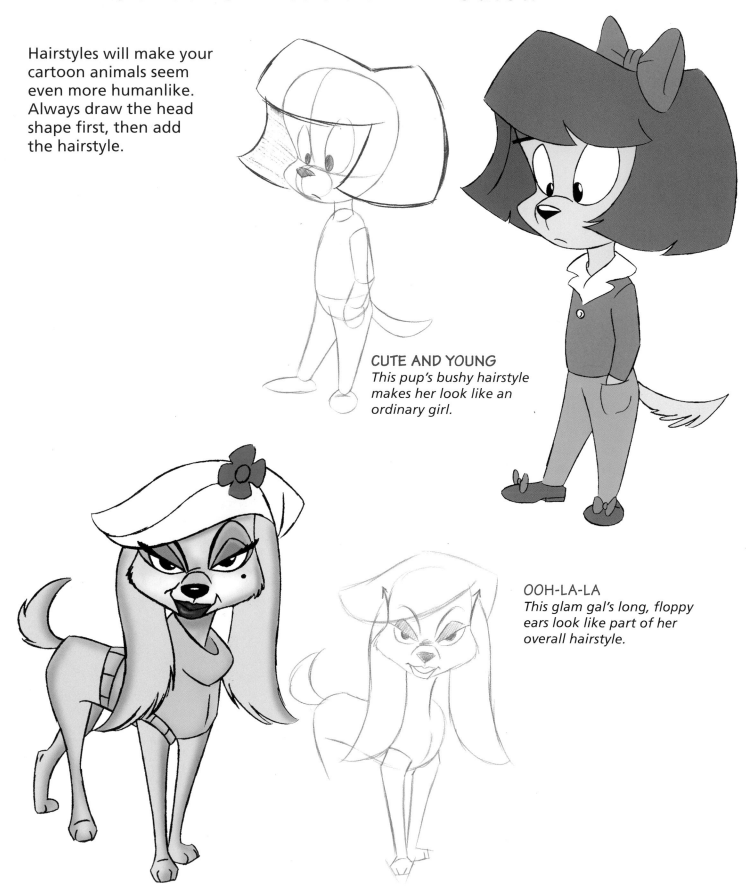

**CUTE AND YOUNG**
*This pup's bushy hairstyle makes her look like an ordinary girl.*

**OOH-LA-LA**
*This glam gal's long, floppy ears look like part of her overall hairstyle.*

SHAGGY

CLEAN CUT

TEENAGER

Here are some fun hairstyles to try. See how many others you can come up with on your own!

BUSHY

TRENDY

# Drawing and Redrawing

When you finish a drawing, take a step back and look at it. Which parts are good and which could be better? This cowboy went through many stages on his way to becoming a finished character.

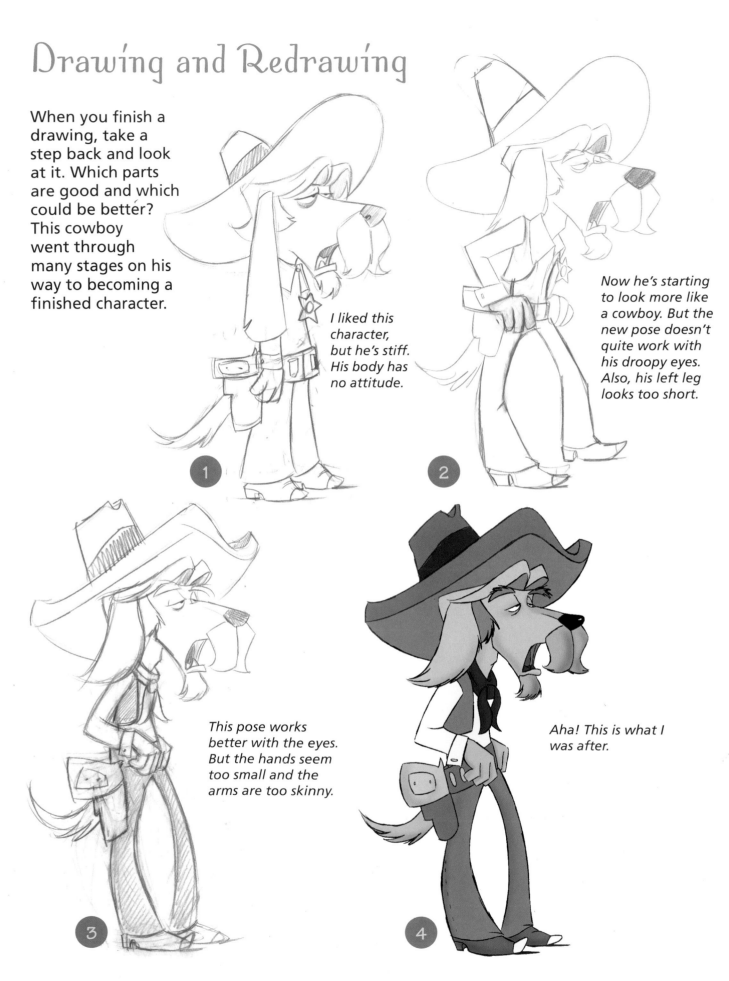

*I liked this character, but he's stiff. His body has no attitude.*

①

*Now he's starting to look more like a cowboy. But the new pose doesn't quite work with his droopy eyes. Also, his left leg looks too short.*

②

*This pose works better with the eyes. But the hands seem too small and the arms are too skinny.*

③

*Aha! This is what I was after.*

④

# Boys and Girls Together

Cartoonists usually draw "boy" dogs as more cartoony, big-nosed, and round and "girl" dogs as more polished and refined. Just look at the difference between the noses on the two dogs below.

# INDEX

alarmed expression, 9
anatomy, 28–31
angry expression, 9

baby dogs, 46
bone structure, 28–31
brainy type, 45
bulldog, 25, 58
bullmastiff, 20
bully type, 44
bumbling type, 53

Chihuahuas, 24
chow chow, 16
clean-cut type, 61
cocker spaniel, 14
collie, 17
costumes, 58–59

Doberman pinscher, 18
dogs
    anatomy, 28–31
    body views, 11–13
    breeds of, 14–27
    ears, 10
    expressions, 9
    head, 6–8
    human posture, 57
    lines, 36–39
    mutts, 47
    running, 33–34

walking, 32, 35
*See also* puppies

ears, 10
embarrassed expression, 9
evil grin, 9

facial expressions, 9, 16, 43
females, 60, 63

gender, indicating, 63
German shepherd, 21
Great Dane, 19
growl, 49

hairstyles, 60–61
happy expression, 9
head, 6–8, 40
hot-tempered type, 54
human posture, 53, 57

jowls, 19, 25

laughing, 9
lines
    of action, 37–38
    flowing, 36
    of spine, 39

Maltese, 23
mischievous type, 43

mudi dog, 27
mutts, 47

personality, 16, 20, 43–45, 54–55, 61
puppies
    babies, 46
    head/body, 40
    personality types, 43–45
    running, 42
    sitting, 41
    *See also* dogs

redrawing, 62
running, 33–34, 42

Saint Bernard, 22
shaggy type, 61
sheepdog, 26
sitting, 41
sneaking pose, 21
snobby expression, 9
sophisticated type, 55
spine line, 39
suspicious expression, 9

teenager, 61
teeth, baring, 49
terriers, 15
trendy type, 61

villainous smile, 51

walking, 32, 35
wolves, 48
    growl, 49
    mangy, 52
    personality types, 53–55
    villainous smile, 51
    in winter, 50
worried expression, 9